THICK BLACK THE

Jonathan Anxin

Copyright 2009, 2015:
Http://www.EarthWaterFireAir.com

Jon Anxin's Introduction

Many people have heard by now of Thick Black Theory.

Written in the early part of the 20th century by Li Zongwu, it imparts the highest strategies for personal power.

If you diligently study Thick Black Theory each day, you will become a modern day hero.

Many scholars say that there are three states or levels that one goes through when studying something intensely.

At the first stage, the road seems extremely long, snaking off into the distance. It just stretches, seemingly forever into the horizon.

As you plod along this road, you become wholly engrossed in your subject.

Fundamental things like eating and sleeping become secondary to you.

In the last stage, you've reached the spot where the horizon was when you first set out.

You take a look back at the road you have traveled and reflect upon your journey.

Then, you realize your original goal was just a mile marker on your unending road to advancement.

The road still stretches far off into the horizon, but you are a wholly different person now.

We offer the first and only translation of Thick Black Theory into the English language.

The study of Thick Black also brings you through three stages.

In the following, I will more closely examine the first level.

The Cost Of Missed Opportunity

In the first stage, your face is as thin as paper.

With friction, it becomes like leather, and at last it becomes as thick as a brick wall.

Your heart starts off red.

As you endure, it gradually becomes white, then gray, then black – and finally black as coal.

Han Xin is widely considered to have been one of the most capable men in history, but when he was young, before he had made a name for himself, all he did was loaf about the city.

One day, he ran into a local thug in the city's busiest market.

The thug said to Han Xin, "I hear you're pretty tough. Well, let's see about that. Get down on the ground and crawl through my legs or I'll take this knife and kill you.".

Hearing the commotion, a crowd started to gather, wanting to see how this scene would play out.

Han Xin thought for a moment, got on his hands and knees, and crawled through the thugs legs right in front of everyone.

In ancient times, that was an incredibly humiliating thing to do.

A big loss of face.

But Han Xin's thinking on the matter was quite simple.

He knew that he wanted to accomplish great things in his life and if he would have killed that thug, then according to the strict Qin laws, he would have had to replace that man's life with his own.

So, after weighing the costs and benefits, he realized it was much better for him to just take the insult, no matter how embarrassing it was at the time.

At this time, Han Xin's face was obviously not as thin as paper.

He had already attained the first level of [Thick Black Theory](#).

Later on in life, Han Xin did end up accomplishing some great things.

During the war between the kingdoms of Chu and Han, there were three exceptional people.

[Liu Bang](#) and [Xiang Yu](#) were the strongest, but Han Xin was in the middle.

If Han Xin was to help Chu, Chu would win the war.

If Han Xin was to aid Han, then the Han kingdom would win.

Han Xin's strategic adviser suggested that Han Xin himself could take the throne if he would try for it.

But at this time, Han Xin's face wasn't thick enough and his heart wasn't black enough.

He didn't take the advice and he decided to help Liu Bang.

Many years later, Liu Bang won the war and established the Han Dynasty.

Many of the generals that helped him win the war felt that Liu Bang hadn't given them what they deserved, and planned a revolt.

Han Xin felt the same way and regretted the fact that he hadn't tried to take the throne himself when he had the chance.

Han Xin and the Generals staged a coup.

He hoped to become the Son Of heaven, but he had

missed the opportunity.

The revolt that Han Xin and the generals staged failed, and Han Xin was assassinated.

We Don't Come Across Many Great Opportunities In Our Lives

When an opportunity shows itself we must grasp it without hesitation.

Han Xin was a smart man.

When he encountered that thug, he knew that he needed to choose his battles, but at the crucial juncture when he had the chance of becoming emperor, he didn't take action.

Instead he deferred to Liu Bang.

He failed to do what would have benefited him the most.

From this we can see that Han Xin reached only the first level of Thick Black Theory. . .

All Masterpieces Were Once Works In Progress

Your life is like a painting.

What others have to say about it is merely a critique.

Some people will like it and others won't.

Their words of praise or censure should not influence the content of the painting. It's your painting. It's your life.

Let's look at a rather extreme example:

Say that someone is born a thief. They are compelled to steal.

They know it's wrong and they know that the whole world condemns them.

They even tried other ways to get by, but despite the hardships associated with it, they are the most comfortable being a thief.

If this person isn't an adherent to Thick Black Theory, then they will have even more problems.

They'll reflect on others criticisms and appraisals and even though they'll still be a thief, they'll be a very unhappy thief.

They will have no sense of self worth.

The paintbrush isn't in their hand. It's in the hand of

another.

The picture on the thief's canvass doesn't belong to him or her.

It was painted by someone else.

I'm not suggesting that becoming a thief is a wise choice. In this example, the person in question is destined to be a thief. That part is not changeable.

What can be changed is how he views his life.

He can be confident in his actions or live a life of second guessing.

Even if you're not a thief, the same applies to you.

People that care too much about face aren't living for themselves.

They are always just struggling to win the approval of others.

The first step towards Thick and Black is completely discarding your "face".

Otherwise, you will have no chance to understand it further.

To Seek Existence Is A Natural Instinct

Li Zongwu said, "to seek existence is a natural instinct."

What he is referring to is the idea of self-preservation – a kind of innate selfishness.

Selfishness, to a degree is natural

For example, if you and another person fall into a rushing river at the same time, what's your first reaction?

What's your instinct, aside from first trying to save yourself?

Those who study Power know that they must insulate themselves from the cold criticisms of others.

By doing this, they can create and maintain a positive self image.

People that are thin skinned and have a soft heart, when attempting to make their dreams a reality, always concern themselves with the appraisals of others.

It is possible that they will reach their goal, but it's also possible that they will give up because they are affected by others opinions.

By catering to the desires of others they get distracted and thrown off the course.

It's much more difficult for them to reach their desired outcome.

People proficient in the use of power are not afflicted with this.

They know that you must learn to put others appraisals to one side.

More importantly, they know they should not change their course of action just to please someone else.

They should never doubt their own ability and value.

People with this kind of attitude will easily enter the ranks of success.

The Enchanting Empress

Let's look at the story of Wu Zetian.

She was the only woman in the history of China to found her own dynasty and take the title of Empress Regnant.

In 636, the Tang Emperor Taizong heard of Wu Zetian's

beauty and summoned her to the palace.

She became a low-level concubine of the emperor.

She was only 14 years old.

Usually, once a girl enters the palace, she will never see her family again – something quite saddening to most.

When they were saying their final goodbyes, her mother was crying bitterly and Wu Zetian asked her, "Why are you crying? How do you know it's not my fate to meet the son of Heaven?".

Wu Zetian viewed her entering the palace as a great opportunity.

She was a precocious girl. She loved to read history and discuss political affairs.

She had a determined and resolute character, and she developed in to an expert of Thick Black Theory.

Emperor Taizong have her the nickname Wumei, "mei" meaning "Enchanting".

While the Emperor knew that she was something special and did favor her at times, there were 3,000 other concubines to contend with and she wasn't quite able to win the Emperors heart.

She had spent 12 years in the palace and hadn't had any children. Wu Zetian hadn't managed to capture the heart of the Emperor, but there was a budding romance between her and Prince Gaozong.

When the emperor was Gravely ill, he suspected Wu Zetian and the Prince might be plotting something so he decided to put her to death.

One day, Prince Gaozong and Wu Zetian were together in front of the bed taking care of Emperor Taizong.

Taizong said to Wu Zetian, "Since I've been ill, the medicine I'm taking has had no effect.

My condition is getting worse and worse every day.

You've taken care of me for so many years, and I just can't bear to throw you away. What do you plan to do after I die?"

Wu Zetian was a master of Thick Black Theory.

She detected the veiled meaning behind the Emperors words and broke out into a cold sweat.

She quickly calmed herself down and said to Taizong, "Before I thought that I should die in order to repay your Majesty.

But it's possible that you may recover from your illness, so I shouldn't die yet either.

I think it's a better way to repay your Majesty to fast and pray for your recovery."

This was a very resourceful answer.

She chose the best road.

Actually the only road that would keep her alive.

Taizong thought for a minute and agreed to this course of action.

While Taizong was still alive, the budding romance between Wu Zetian and Gaozong started to blossom. But things always have a way of changing.

The following year, Taizong passed away.

According to the customs of the times, all of the consorts who did not bear children had to go to Ganye Temple and become nuns, including Wu Zetian.

On an anniversary of Taizong's death, Emperor Gaozong went to Ganye Temple to offer incense and prayers.

When he and Wu Zetian saw each other, it was very clear that the flame of their previous romance had not been extinguished.

She immediately recognized this and grasped this opportunity.

She spoke with him and started reminiscing about the times they had shared together.

Emperor Gaozong took her back to the palace with him.

Return To The Palace

This second time entering the palace Wu Zetian was already 28 years old.

While she was still attractive, she could not compete with the 19 year old concubines on physical beauty.

She, however was unmatched in experience and cunning.

She had plenty of Thick Black tricks up her sleeve.

She knew she already had a history with Emperor Gaozong and if she maneuvered correctly she could win his heart.

At this time, Emperor Gaozong did not favor Empress Wang as she had not born any children.

He much favored his concubine Consort Xiao who had one son, Li Sujie and two daughters – Princess Yiyang and Xuancheng.

Empress Wang, seeing that emperor Gaozong was still impressed by Wu Zetian's beauty hoped that the arrival of a new concubine would divert the Emperor's attention from Consort Xiao, so Empress Wang was very good to Wu Zetian.

In turn, Wu Zetian was very respectful to the Empress.

In addition, the Empress and Wu Zetian joined forces to force Consort Xiao out of the picture and since Wu Zetian was liked by the Emperor and Empress she quickly moved up to "Zhaoyi", the highest ranking concubine.

But remember – Wu Zetian was an expert of Thick Black Theory She wasn't satisfied with just being the top concubine.

She had her eyes on the position of Empress.

She waited until her position as "Zhaoyi" was solidified, then started implementing her plan.

By this time she had four sons and two daughters with the emperor.

Her second born was an extremely cute girl who the Empress liked very much.

One day, right after the Empress came to see the little girl, Wu Zetian poisoned her own daughter.

When the Emperor came and found his daughter dead, he was sure it was Empress Wang who killed her out of jealousy.

So, with the execution of this plan Wu Zetian disposed of Empress Wang and captured the title of Empress herself.

From the time she entered the palace until the time she became Empress, she didn't really have especially good luck.

All of her success was a direct result of her precise planning.

She implemented her Thick Black gongfu very well.

In order to attack Empress Wang, she even killed her own daughter.

It's very difficult to compare her "thickness" and "blackness".

She kept focused on the result she wanted despite the occasional setbacks and finally achieved her goal.

This is an extreme example and I wouldn't suggest that people go around killing their own children.

But from this example we can glean a sense of the "spirit" of Thick Black.

Everyone Has The Power To Decide Their Own Fate

Wu Zetian was a poor peasant and she managed to become the only female Emperor in the history of China.

She is a classic example of how someone can change their own fate.

Even though some people abdicate this power, we hold our lives in our own hands.

Therefore, the first step to enter the Temple of Thick and Black is to put yourself at the center.

The path to all your needs and wants starts from within.

As long as you maintain this mindset, the criticism of others can't disrupt your operations.

As your grip strengthens on the paintbrush, you gradually become Thicker and Blacker.

You become the Master of Yourself.

Who was Li Zongwu?

Many people are curious these days about Li Zongwu, the inventor of Thick Black Theory.

Who was he? Nan Huaidong relates his experience of Li Zongwu:

I left Zhejiang for Chengdu. I had just turned 20 years old. People in Chengdu weren't too fond of people from Zhejiang, but I wanted to study Feijian kung-fu and fight the Japanese army.

So, I often visited people who were famous, well-educated and had a lot of kung-fu skill and knowledge.

In Chengdu at the time, there were a lot of tea houses in Shaocheng Park.

Brew a pot of tea, sit for half the day or the whole day and pay when you left.

If you had to leave at some point to run some errands, you could leave and just put the lid on your cup up-side down, the owner of the shop would leave it until you got back.

If you didn't have any money to drink tea, that was okay too.

When the boss asked you what you wanted, you just told them I'll have a glass.

And they would bring you a glass of water.

I don't think we'll see this kind of rural relaxed atmosphere ever again.

Shaocheng Park was a the place to gather for many famous people and many people that still followed older traditions.

You could often see people wearing long qipaos and cloth shoes.

These were just the type of people I was looking for, so I often went there.

To the people there, I was just a kid.

I wore Sun Yat Sen style suits and I was from Zhejiang-- the place Chang Kai Shek was from.

People were suspicious of me at first.

Maybe I was sent out to Chengdu by Chang Kai Shek.

After a while, people slowly began to understand.

I was out there to learn.

The suspicion faded and I began to make friends.

One day, I was at Chengshao Park with some friends drinking tea and playing chess.

A man walked in. He was tall, hunched over and wearing a felt cap.

He had an interesting look--he looked like someone from ancient times.

When he came in, everyone nodded and said hello.

I asked my friend Mr. Liang who it was. He told me that it was the father of Thick Black Theory Li Zongwu and that he was quite famous in Sichuan.

Then Mr. Liang told me Li Zongwu's story. I wanted to meet him.

So, Mr. Liang took me over there and introduced me.

The father of Thick Black Theory invited us to sit down and have some tea and chat.

Our so-called chat consisted of us sitting there and listening to him expound his theories of this and that, talk about the Japanese occupation, listen to him curse the Sichuan Army and listen to him talk about how this and that person were worthless.

This was my first meeting, but after I would see him often in Chengshao Park.

One time he said to me, "I can see that you want to make a name for yourself--become a hero.

I can teach you a way that will make it happen much faster.

If you want to succeed and make a name for yourself

you should curse people, that's what I did.

And you don't need to curse a lot of people, just curse me.

Say 'That Li Zongwu is a bastard. He should die.' And you'll succeed.

But you need to stick a note extolling Confucius on your forehead while you do so.

And in your mind honor me Li Zongwu as the god of Thick and Black."

I didn't take his advice and thus didn't make a name for myself.

Another time when I was talking to him, I told him that he doesn't need to talk about Thick Black Theory anymore and he doesn't need to curse people anymore.

He turned and said to me, "I'm not just cursing people at random."

Everyone has a 'thick face.' I'm only taking that false face and peeling it off.

I told him that he needs to be careful and that there are people in the central government that are noticing him.

There he might get taken to jail.

He replied, "My boy, you don't understand. I'm the same age as Einstein."

Einstein invented the Theory of Relativity and now he is a world famous scientist.

But I'm here in Sichuan, in Chengdu and I haven't really made a name for myself.

I hope they catch me. If they throw me in jail, then I'll be world famous."

He was never taken to jail and he didn't become world famous.

Later he said that it was bad luck.

But that year, his book was very popular all across China.

A lot of people were a bit scared of him after that, but not me.

I still talked to him quite often.

A couple years later, a friend of mine, a monk, had passed away.

My friend, also a monk, and I wanted to go to Zilongjing to pay our respects.

We traveled for eight days. When we found the friend's grave, we bowed our heads and burned incense.

At the time, I hadn't realized how far away Zilongjing was from Chengdu. It would be another eight days to get back.

It dawned on me that I wouldn't have enough money to get back.

I started to get very worried.

Then I remember that Li Zongwu was from Zilongjing.

And he was a famous person, so I was sure that anyone I asked would know where his house was.

We began walking and asked around.

His house was quite big and the front gate was wide open. Before it was always like that in the countryside.

The front gate was opened in the morning and not shut until night.

Not like how it is in the big cities these days.

We walked in and called his name.

He came right away and he seemed very happy to see me.

"Where did you come from? What are you doing out here?"

I came to visit a friend of mine who passed away.

But I'm not dead yet!

After the brief misunderstanding was cleared up, he arranged for dinner to be prepared.

After the meal and some drinks I told him that there was another reason I was there to see him.

I told him that I didn't have enough money to get back to Chengdu.

He asked how much I needed and I told him that I needed ten dollars.

He got up and went to a cabinet in the living room and got and envelope and gave it to me.

There was twenty dollars in there. I told him that I only needed ten.

He insisted that I take twenty. I told him that I didn't know when I would be able to pay him back.

He said to spend the money first, then figure it out.

We chatted for a bit and he suddenly suggested that I don't return to Chengdu, that I stayed there for a while.

"Stay here and do what?" I asked.

"Don't you like kung-fu? There is a guy named Master Zhao in this town who has excellent kung-fu skills.

He was born a cripple, but his kung-fu is still very good, especially his soft-style.

He can put on a pair of new shoes and walk a mile in the snow and there won't be a speck of mud on them.

He once had a disciple that learned kung-fu pretty well but misused what he had learned.

One night the disciple crept over a wall into a family's house and raped a woman, so Master Zhao had to kill him.

And after that he hasn't taken on any more students.

It's a shame that someone with such good skills won't

pass them on to anyone.

But with my recommendation I think he would take you on as a student. If you train with him for three years, you will be a master yourself."

I told him that I would go back to my lodging and think about it.

Early the next morning, Li Zongwu met us at our lodge and continued with the idea of me training with Master Zhao.

He said that he would even pay for those three years of study for me.

But I had decided that three years was too long.

I went back to Chengdu.

Not long after, I heard news of Li Zonwu's passing.

He died of natural causes. I was quite sad.

I thought of him lending me the money and his offering to pay for my kung-fu studies, this father of Thick Black Theory didn't seem to be very Thick and Black at all.

He actually seemed quite sincere.

Enjoy the material herein, and benefit from it. Study and spread Thick Black Theory.

—   Jon Anxin

Introduction

When I read the history of China, I found a lot of flaws.

I think the judgments of the risen and fallen - the success and failure of the "24 histories", are completely wrong.

The truth that sages spoke is not right, also.

I was surprised.

The successful people from ancient times must have had some secret, which was unseen by the sages.

I was frustrated because I tried so hard but could find no answer.

Once, when I was thinking about the three kingdoms, I realized that the simple secret is nothing more than "Thick Face" and "Black Heart".

Then, I read the 24 histories again. Those four words are really included.

Then I wrote the book "Thick Black Theory" with simple words.

It had 3 parts. They are:

- Thick Black Theory
- Thick Black Scripture
- Spread and Study of Thick Black

In 1912, it was published by the Public Daily in Chengdu.

At that time, this new theory made a big commotion with the readers.

Before the second part was published, I stopped because my friend persuaded me to.

But after that, the 3 words "Thick Black Theory" became common nouns.

Every time I went somewhere, I was always asked to make speeches about Thick Black Theory, so I told all the details.

The audiences all nodded their heads and sighed – "I failed because I didn't do things in a thick and black way" . . .

Some said, "He was successful because he knew it to well."

Sometimes, when I met some strangers, after we exchanged names he looked at me with an amazed look. "Are you the person who invented Thick Black Theory?"

Or people introduced me to others as the inventor of Thick Black Theory.

What's more funny, is when students write essays, they used it like it's a common thing.

Then I realized how popular this became.

I wrote it as some kind of fun game at first, but didn't expect it to become so effective.

I'm surprised myself, too. The reason why people like it is a psychological reason.

Then I kept studying, I realized Thick Black Theory is from the "Total Depravity Theory".

It has the same value as the "Total Goodness Theory" of Wang Yang Ming's literature "To The Conscious".

The ancients said: "Kindheartedness and justice are in everyone's nature."

But I say "Thick Black is in everyone's nature."

Yangming said, "We knew filial piety when we met our fathers.

We knew honor when we met our brothers."

He was so sure about that.

I say "little babies grab their mother's food and put it in their own mouths when they see it.

The babies push their brothers away when they see them coming while they are eating." And I'm sure about that, too.

People love Yangming . . .

So they love Thick Black Theory, too.

There was the "Total Goodness Theory" from Mencius, so Xun Zi had his "Total Depravity Theory" to fight against it.

There was "To the Conscious" from Wang Yangming, so I have "Thick Black Theory", too.

What are people's natures all about?

I really want to figure it out.

I read so many theories from the Song, Yuan, Ming, and Qing Dynasty but most of them are disconnected, boring, and difficult to understand.

Then I threw the books away and tried to study

psychology as physics, because I think they are connected in some way.

We can tell if human nature is good or bad — just like we can't tell if fire and water are good or bad.

Mencius' Total Goodness and Xunzi's Total Depravity are sideways opinions, and the Thick Black Theory I'm talking about is more sideways, just like Wang Yangming's "To the Conscious".

If you don't understand, no matter how thick and black you try to be, it would fail anyway.

You will understand if you read "psychology and dynamics" of mine.

Even if we don't want to be thick and black, we should be careful about other people being thick and black to us, so we have to understand the tricks.

Thick And Black Theory

Since I learned to read, I wanted to be a hero.

I searched in "four books and five scripts", and got nothing.

I looked in hundreds of sorts of literary schools, and I still got nothing.

But I believed there must be some secret to being a hero.

I didn't find out just because I was dumb.

I searched so hard for years, and didn't care about anything except finding it.

Once, when I was thinking about the three kingdoms, I suddenly realized – all the heroes in history have nothing more than Thick Face and Black Heart.

Amongst the heroes during the three kingdoms, the first is [Cao Cao](#).

His personality was all black heart. He killed Lu Boshe, killed Kong Rong, killed Yang Xiu, Killed Dong Chengfuwan.

Then he killed the queen and the prince. He dared to do anything.

He even said "I'd rather betray everyone in the world instead of others betraying me."

His heart was so black that nobody could ever reach it. That's why he became a hero on top at that time.

The second one should be [Liu Bei](#).

It was all about thick face in his personality.

He depended on Cao Cao, depended on Lu Bu, depended on Liu Biao, depending on Cun Qan, depended on Yuan Shao.

He went to so many places, lived in other people's houses – and didn't feel ashamed about it.

And he liked crying all throughout his life.

In the stories of the three kingdoms it was portrayed so vividly.

He cried to everyone when he met problems he couldn't solve.

Then, the failure became an achievement.

So people said "Liu Bei cried his kingdom up". It's also an ability.

Cao Cao and he were absolutely on the top of thick and black.

They were talking about heroes while boiling wine.

One had the most black heart, one had the thickest face – but they both couldn't help it.

We can see all the people around them.

They all were not thick and black enough.

That's why Cao Cao said to Liu Bei, "There are only two heroes in the world. Me and you."

There was another one. Sun Quan. He was the confederate of Liu Bei and he was one of Liu Bei's relatives.

Suddenly he killed Guan Yu and occupied Jin Zhou state.

His heart was almost as black as Cao Cao's – They were both top heroes.

He told Cao Cao that he was Cao Cao's minister. His face was almost as thick as Liu Bei's.

He was neither black as Cao Cao nor thick as Liu Bei but he had the two skills, so he was one of the heroes, too.

They all couldn't conquer any of the others kingdoms even if they tried their best to fight.

That's why the country was separated into 3 parts.

After Cao Cao, Liu Bei, and Sun Quan all died one after another, Sima seized the opportunity and rose up.

He learned from Cao, Liu, and others and became the most thick and black person.

He could tease widows and orphans.

As black as Cao Cao.

He could take a woman's insult. His face was even thicker than Liu Bei's.

When I read the story that Sima Yi was insulted by a woman, I was so surprised.

"That's why the world was Sima's." The country had to be united by him.

It's a case of "The present being caused by little things in the past."

Zhuge Liang was a genius in the country, but when he met Sima Yi he couldn't deal with him.

He even determined to "do his best to fight until the end of his life."

But he didn't get a piece of the land of central China until he died from vomiting blood.

Even the best general of the king couldn't defeat the

thick and black enemy.

I studied the stories of the few great people, and found out the mystical secret.

A series of 24 histories can be explained with "Thick and Black".

Let me show you more proof with the history of the Han dynasty.

Xiang Yu was a hero who could lift a mountain, and who could cover the sky.

Thousands of people died when he shouted, but why did he die in the east city and get laughed at by the world?

The reason why he failed – it's like what Han Xin said, "Women's kindness and men's braveness".

It included everything. Women are kind because they can't take the cruel things around.

As his heart wasn't black.

Men are brave because they can't take other people's insult, as their faces are not thick.

In the story of the Hongmen feast, Xiang Yu and Liu

Bang were sitting together.

Xiang Yu already took the sword out. What he needed to do was just push it into Liu Bang – then he could be emperor right away.

But he hesitated and didn't do anything and allowed Liu Bang to escape.

In the story of the failure in Gaixia, if he could go over Wujiang river, and did things right from the beginning, he could have been the winner.

But he said, "Eight thousand people of this land went over the river to the west.

Nobody came back today but this land and the people love me and treat me so well – how can I sit here and not feel guilt about it?"

All these talks were so wrong!

He said he couldn't lose his face.

He said he was guilty for what he had done.

How can the heroes be right all the time?

How can they say they are guilty?

He didn't realize it and said, "God wants me to die. It's not because of the war."

I'm afraid he should not have blamed God.

Let's get deeper into Liu Bang's stories.

In history, Xiang Yu asked Han emperor (Liu Bang), "The world has been a mess with wars and fighting for years – except us.

I'd like to challenge and have a fight with you."

Han emperor smiled, "I'd rather fight with intelligence than fight with strength."

Do you know why he smiled?

When Liu Bang me Li Sheng, Liu had two girls wash his feet. Li Sheng blamed him for disrespecting his elder, then he fell on his knees and asked for forgiveness.

His father was in great danger, but he still wanted to get something from him.

Even his own children – Xiaohui and Luyuan, when the army of Chu almost caught them – he pushed them off the carriage and then he killed Han Xin, and Peng Yue.

"Put up the gun after all the birds are killed.

Eat the hound after all the rabbits are killed" (Kill the helpers after you succeed).

So what on earth was Liu Bang thinking about?

How could Xiang Yu understand, who was a man with "women's kindness and men's braveness"?

In the history book of Sima, it said Liu Bang had a face of a dragon (with a long nose).

Xiang Yu had double pupils (2 pupils in each eye), but it said nothing about if they have thick face or black heart.

It's a pity.

Liu Bang's face and heart were different from other peoples.

They can be called the saints from heaven.

But his heart was so black like he was born with black nature.

Everything he did could never depart from blackness and his thick face was based on some "diploma".

His teacher was Zhang Liang, one of the "three most talented".

Zhang Liang's teacher was the Bridge Old Man.

We can easily find in the historical documents about them teaching and learning.

In the story that Zhang Liang met an old man on the bridge he was actually teaching him to have a thick face.

Su Dongpo commented on this story and showed this clearly, too.

Zhang Liang was a smart person.

After he was given the direction he understood.

That's why the old man expected him as a teacher of the emperor.

This kind of teaching cannot be understood by the dumb people.

In history, "Liang taught a lot of people, but nobody really learned except Liu Bang."

Liang said Liu Bang was a "student from God".

We can see that this kind of ability is like "For a smart person, the good teachers would be scarce, but it's even harder to find good students".

When Han Xin asked to be Qi emperor, Li Bang almost blew his top, but his teacher Zhang Liang pointed him in the right direction.

Just as the teachers correcting the students fault in the schools now.

Even a person who was smart like Liu Bang could sometimes make mistakes.

We can imagine how deep this study is.

Liu Bang was smart and well-learned.

He broke the 5 relationship moralities — "King and the minister, father and son, brothers, husband and wife, friends" . . .

He even wiped out all proprieties and humilities so he could root out all the heroes and unite the country for the next 400 years.

The system of his family was beginning to fade out.

During the time of the Chu Han period, there was someone who had the thickest face, but no black heart. He failed in the end. Who is he?

It's Han Xin.

He could crawl between someone's legs – His face wasn't thinner than Liu Bang's.

But he didn't pay much attention to the black.

When he was the Qi emperor, if he listened to Kuai Tong it would have been awesome but he was thinking about Liu Bang's favor for him.

He said, "Wear his clothes, should think about his worries. Eat his food, should get killed for him".

Then his head was cut off by Liu Bang. Even his family were all killed but he deserved that.

Liu Bang laughed about his kindness and braveness.

He knew this rule clearly, but he didn't follow it.

According to the studies about, Thick Black Theory looks simple, ut it's subtle when you use it.

Use a little and you see a little effect.

Use a lot, and you'll see a huge impact.

Liu Bang and Sima Yi learned it.

They united the country.

Cao Cao and Liu Bei had each of them and still somewhat succeeded.

Han Xin and Fang Zeng also learned one part but they lived in the wrong times with the thickest and blackest Liu Bang.

That is why they all failed.

But before they died they still became some kind of minister or general.

They were outstanding once and after they died, they were still remembered by people.

Then we talked about them.

We still respect them.

It's the power of Thick and Black.

God gave us lives, with a face which was thick, with a heart which was black.

It looks normal on the surface but if you investigate it deeply, you would know that there's no end for black and thick.

Peoples' wealth, desires, nice clothes and cars all come

from this.

What the creator made is fantastic.

There are so many dumb people who don't know about it, but the dumbest people are those who know there is a way but don't use it.

Thick Black Theory has 3 parts: The 1st is "thick as the wall, black as the coal".

The skin of the face is like a piece of paper at the beginning, and it's getting thicker and thicker.

Then it becomes as thick as the wall.

The color of the heart was red. It becomes darker and darker and then it's black like coal in the end.

But it's just the first step, because no matter how thick the wall is, it can still be destroyed by a cannon.

The coal is black, so people won't want to get close to it.

So it's just a basic skill.

The 2nd step is "thick and hard, black and bright".

The people who are good at being thick – no matter

how hard you strike them, they don't move at all.

Liu Bei was this kind of person. Even Cao Cao didn't have any way to beat him.

When people are black like a blackboard, the more black it is the more people will like it.

Cao Cao was like that. He was the famous black heart person.

He made all the talented people want to join him.

If you reach the 2nd step, it could be so different than the 1st step, but you can still see the mark when you pay attention to look.

Just like we can see Cao Cao's heart so clearly.

The 3rd step is "thick but no trace, Black but no color".

So thick and so black. Up to the heavens, down to the earth.

Nobody can see it's thick or black. It's so hard to reach that level.

We could only find it amongst the saints.

People asked, "How can it be so intense?"

I said, "The moderation of confusion . . .

We can only stop until it has no sound or smell.

The Buddhist can only stop until there is nothing there because there is nothing in the mind.

That can only be called success.

"As Thick Black Theory is a deep secret theory, no shape and no color should be above it."

Anyway, until now emperors, generals, premiers, heroes and saints – the successful people were all thick or black.

History has been written.

The facts can't be changed.

You should search it with the directions I gave you.

You will find the true path to success.

Thick and Black Scripture

Li Zongwu said, "it's thick if it's not thin. It's black if it's not white."

This is the true law from people in history.

I'm afraid this will be forgotten by people after a long time, so I wrote it down and told people.

This book talks about thick and black at first.

It talks about everything in the universe in the middle.

And talks about thick and black again in the end.

It can be used on everything in the universe, but they can be hidden behind faces and hearts.

It's what you should learn carefully. Those who are good at understanding can use and get benefit all their lives.

It's called Thick and Black for destiny.

Making thick and black practical is called study.

Studying thick and black is called moralization.

People can leave thick and black any time.

If you leave it, it's not thick and black anymore.

So men should be careful and afraid if their faces and hearts are not thick and black enough.

Nothing is more dangerous than a thin face and a good heart.

Never showing any real expression is thick.

Showing everything without any doubt is black.

Thick is the nature of the world.

Black is the truth of the world.

You have both thick and black, and the world will be afraid of you and you won't fear any evil or good.

Li Zongwu told the secret of people in history to set up the issue. He said thick and black are the nature that you can't change.

Actually thick and black are already part of people.

Then he told us the importance of being thick and black, and at last he talked about the great benefit of thick and black.

If you make the decision to study thick and black theory and use your own experience to feel it – to erase the moral stuff you have learned in your life so you can understand thick and black theory more clearly.

This is the main point of this book. Li Zongwu's words are quoted in the rest of the chapters.

Zongwu said, "The theory of thick and black is easy and hard.

It's easy because normal people can understand it, but it's hard because even Cao and Liu didn't understand deeply."

Zongwu said, "People say my heart is black but put me in the coal – they are still different.

People say my face is thick – but it can still be hurt with a knife."

Zongwu said, "Thick and black theory can be tested in society.

It can be proven with the 3 emperors stories (Yao, Shun, Yu). It won't be wrong.

It's reasonable in the world. It's approved by the ghosts and gods.

It will still be right after hundreds of years."

Zongwu said, "People work on the basic idea.

Once the basic ideas are approved, they become the path.

Shouldn't thick and black be a basic idea?"

Zongwu said, "Three people walking together . . .

There must be one who can be my teacher.

I choose the thick and black one to teach and improve me."

Zongwu said, "God gave me thick and black ability.

What can humans do to me?"

Zongwu said, "Even at a small place with ten families there must be someone who is thick and black like Li Zongwu.

They just don't say it."

Zongwu said, "Great people won't leave Thick Black Theory even when they are having dinner.

They will stay with thick and black no matter how busy they are. No matter how bad their situations are."

Zongwu said, "If there was someone with Xiang Yu's talent and ability who had thick face and black heart – The people like Liu Bang wouldn't even be worth talking about.

Zongwu said, "The thick and black people can have an empire with thousands of chariots.

The others can't even get a bowl of rice."

Zongwu said, "Cereals are good plants for people, but the raw ones are useless like weeds.

It's definitely important to make thick and black ripe."

Zongwu said, "the teachers who teach about Taoism are bad to our Thick Black Theory.

They look honest, faithful, and they do things right and good.

Everyone likes them and they think they are right.

They are not the kind of people who can talk about Cao Cao or Liu Bei's things."

Zongwu said, "it's not strange that people are not thick

and black!

Even the toughest plant can't live after days of strong sunshine, days of freezing.

I found that the people who talk about thick and black are not so many! The good people are going to come up if I quit! Who am I to a good person?

The theory of thick and black today is not a small thing.

You won't understand it until you focus on it."

Li Zongwu is the person who invented Thick Black Theory.

If he had 2 students, one listened and learned very carefully.

The other one learned too, but he was afraid the good people would come and get him, so he always wanted to be a saint to other people.

Now we will see they are learning at the same time, but he can't reach as far as the other can.

Is it because one is smarter? Of course not."

Zongwu said, "If you have failed something, smart people would think:

It must be because my face wasn't thick enough.

After he thought, his face would become thicker but he still failed.

He would think: It must be because my heart wasn't black enough.

Then his heart would get more and more black.
But he still failed.

He would say, The one who was always against me was just a beast!

So what's so hard if I kill it with Thick Black Theory?"

Zongwu said, "the theory of thick and black – isn't it deep and beautiful?

Just like walking far away, you should start from somewhere closer.

Climbing a high mountain, you should start from somewhere
lower.

If you are not thick and black, you can't make your children to be tough.

If you don't use thick and black on other people, you can't make your children listen to you."

The thick and black scripture I wrote is for the people who just learned a bit.

It's easier to read in case they forget.

But there is something really deep, so I wrote some explanation around the scripture.

Zongwu said, "You say it's not thick – it can't be ground thinner.

You say it's not black – it can't be washed white." I changed it into, "you say it's not thick – the more you grind, the thicker it becomes. You say it's notblack – the more you wash the darker it becomes."

Someone said, there is nothing like this.

I said, "The callus on your hands. It can be thicker if you grind it more. The coal with dirt on it."

It can only be darker if you wash it.

People have a thin face at the beginning.

The more they try in society, the thicker their face will be.

People have black hearts in the first place, but it's covered with moral stuff so it doesn't look black. And if we wash it, we can see the black nature.

Zongwu said, "Thick and black are not given by the surroundings.

Everyone has it.

The normal people are all thick or black.

It's just people's nature."

This can be tested.

Find a random mother with a baby in her arms who is eating something in a bowl.

The baby will grab that bowl.

If the mother has a pie in her hand, the baby is going to grab that pie and even grab the part which is already in her mouth and eat it.

Or the baby is in the mother's arms drinking milk when his brother came to him.

He would push him away.

These are all "ability without learning, without thinking".

When you try to do this no matter where or when, you would make a difference.

The Tang dynasty emperor Li Shimin killed his older brother Jiancheng and his younger brother Yuanji.

Even all Jiangcheng and Yuanji's sons, and took all their wives for himself, and forced his father to give him the whole country.

He was using that kind of ability on everything.

But normal people don't think about using it on other things.

He did it, so he became a hero for the whole of history.

So Zongwu said, "Flavor to the mouth is called tasting.

Sound to the ear is called listening. Colors to the eyes is called looking.

And what's to the heart? What has something to do with heart?

It's called thick and black.

So heroes put it to faces and hearts."

The theory of thick and black is so clearly shown in everyone's face but many people are scared or persuaded by the "good people".

So Zongwu said, "The mountain which is used to farm the cows was cut by axes.

It's not unharmed.

The cows and sheep depend on the plants, so both the animals and the plants are killed."

There are always some people in the world who are thick and black.

You try to stop it.

It's just like when people cut the plants – thick and black will be gone.

So it will be extremely hard to have a hero!

People know there is no hero, but they don't know it's because there is no thick and black anymore.

How dramatic it is! If we keep it, then we will have thick and black in the future.

If we don't keep it, it will be gone soon."

Zongwu said, "When kids see their mothers have food in their mouths, they just grab it and eat it, but people don't usually use it much.

That's why people can't be heroes.

That is, the great people always keep their real nature from their childhoods, and people usually give up their nature, called – self abandonment."

Some people who are very smart understand the theory and do it without telling anyone.

And some other people who are not so smart go on the way already, but they don't know what it is.

So Zongwu said, "Know it but don't say it.

Do it but don't know it.

For all their lives they still don't know thick and black is such a common thing."

All the theories in the world can mislead people, but thick and black theory never misleads you.

Even when you don't have anything as a beggar, you

can still get more food than others.

So Zongwu said, "From a president to a beggar, Thick Black Theory can help you.

Thick black theory is deep and hard. If you want to use it really well, you have to study hard, and you can use it after a year. You can do something big after 3 years.

So Zongwu said, "Those who want to learn Thick Black Theory will understand it after months, but can make a difference after 3 years."

Thick And Black Learning

Some people asked me, "You invented Thick Black Theory, but why did you lose doing anything?

Why are your students a lot better than you are?

Even until they tricked or cheated on you?"

I said, "You are wrong. All the inventors can't do very well in the thing they invent.

Confucianism was invented by Confucius.

He became the best about it, and all his students were not better than him.

They all had lower knowledge.

That's because the master is too good about it.

But the Western science is different. It was simple at the beginning, and the more people that studied, the deeper and better it became.

The person who invented the steam machine – he only knew steam can push up the lid.

The one who found electricity only knew that dead frog moved with an electric shock.

And people after made more and more machines with it.

The ancestors never thought of it.

The thing with Western science is that the younger people do better than the older people.

My Thick Black Theory is more like Western science.

I can only talk about pushing up the lid and dead frogs moving.

A lot of theories will be discovered after me, and my students must be better than me.

When I meet them, I will lose for sure.

After they have their own students, their students will beat them also.

Generation after generation Thick Black Theory will go on the right way!"

Some asked me, "You are talking so well about Thick Black Theory – Why didn't you do something big?"

I said, "I have a question. What did Confucius do?

He talked about doing things for the government, for the country.

How many things did he do?

Zeng Zi wrote "Da Xue" (Great Knowledge).

It was about how to manage the country and make it peaceful, but what did he do to manage the country?

What did he do to make it peaceful?

Zi Si wrote "Zhong Yong".

It was about staying the same, trying to adapt to the environment, and making no difference.

Why did he say that?

Why didn't you doubt it?

It's hard to meet a teacher who knows something clearly.

This is "The delicate way that there is nothing else above it, that you can't meet it no matter how many things you will go through".

You doubt so much about it. Don't fool yourself.

When I published Thick Black Theory, many people said, "Thick Black Theory is too deep and hard to understand.

Please show me a shortcut."

Then I asked them, "What do you want to do?"

He said, "I want to be a governor of something, and I want to do something big, and other people would think I'm a man who is in charge of big things."

Then I told him the 6 true words to ask to be a governor or officer.

6 true words to be an officer or governor, and 2 good ways to do things.

The 6 true words to get a position of a governor or officer:

"Free, Dig, Lie, Greasiness, Threaten, Give."

Free
It means: One is about affairs.

The people who want to be a governor or officer have to put away everything.

No job. No business. No farming. No trading – don't

even read or teach.

Just do one thing – ask to be it.

Another is about time. People who want to be a governor or officer have to be patient.

No hurries.

It didn't work today, so do it tomorrow.

It didn't work this year, so do it next year.

Dig
The people who want to be a governor or officer have to dig.

Everyone knows that, but it's hard to define.

Some say "Dig" means dig wherever there is a hole.

I say it's just half right. Dig means dig when there is a whole, and dig when there is nothing.

I define it as: Dig no matter where.

Dig it deeper when there is a hole.

Dig a new one when there is nothing.

Lie
Lie to everyone you can think of.

To your boss or the public.

Orally or on the paper about your ability and talent.

Greasiness
It means flattery. I think everyone knows what it's about.

Threaten
Threaten. There's no harm to talk more about it.

Some people pay so much attention to "greasiness" but it still doesn't work.

It's because they don't threaten.

Once you are a big man, you have to be careful about what you are scared of.

Just a hint – they will give you whatever you want.

You have to know that greasiness goes with threatening.

Other people think that every word you say to them is all about flattery, but actually – it's also some hint to find what they're scared of.

The people who are good at greasiness can make people happy even when it sounds like you are criticizing them.

This is something you have to study deeply.

What's most important is when you threaten them, don't over use it, or they are going to blow their top.

You can even put yourself in
hell.

Don't use "threaten" until you have got nothing else to do.

Give
It means bribes. There are 2 kinds of bribes:

Big bribes, like packs of money, and small bribes, like some wine or little things like asking them to go to dinner.

There are 2 kinds of people who you need to bribe.

The people who have rights and power to use it to help, and the people who will give their position to you.

You will see the miracle if you have done what the 6 words tell you.

Some big man sits there and talks to himself, "Someone wants to have some title.

He talked so much about it (here is "free), he has something to do with me (dig), this person is smart (lie), and he treats me well (greasiness).

But he is a bit bad. If I don't deal with it, he might do something not good for me (threaten), so now he turns around and sees a bunch of something lying on the table (give), he can say nothing more and asks someone to give you some position.

Now you should have gotten all that you want.

Then take up and do what the 6 words below tell you."

The 6 true words to learn to hold power as a governer or officer:

"Empty, Compliment, Tight, Evil, Deaf, Get."

The meanings of the six words:

Empty
Empty means: First is on the paper, when you write or sign some documents.

They should all be empty.

It's hard to explain this.

You can go to all kinds of government offices and read the stuff on the wall or paper. You will understand.

Second is about things. Whatever you do, you should make sure it either can be left or right.

Sometimes you make it fast and strict, but there is a path where you can walk away.

Never make it have anything to do with you when it becomes difficult.

Compliment
Complement means bend your knees, cringe and smile obsequiously.

You can do it directly to your boss, or indirectly to the friends or family of your boss.

Tense
Tense is the opposite of compliment. You do it to them who are lower than you.

First is your appearance.

Make yourself like a saint who can't be offended.

Second is your talk.

You should talk like you are really knowledgeable.

But sometimes you can be obsequious to the lower people, and be tense to the higher.

You need to learn it by yourself, and make it flexible.

Evil
Do whatever you can to reach your purpose.

Kill him, sell his kids.

Don't worry about anything, but there is something you have to be careful about:

You should do every evil thing with a cover of morality.

Deaf
Be deaf to something you don't want to hear.

Just be yourself and do whatever you need to.

And it can also be blind. Be blind if you don't' want to see it.

Get
It means getting money. All the 11 words above are for this one.

Get compares to give above, get comes after give.

But you have to get something done before you get.

If you can't get it done, some money should be given.

The 12 words I talked about are just an outline.

Most of the spirit is not told yet.

You can follow the outline and go study for yourself.

Two good ways of dealing with things

Arrow cutting way
Someone got shot by the arrow and went to see a doctor.

The doctor cut off the parts outside, then asked for the money.

Why didn't he take it out?

He said, "It's a surgeon's job. Go find one."

This is an old story.

Nowadays the people in the governments and the offices all use these ways to deal with things.

Like "This situation is not a part of our job, please go to xx department to find someone else who is in charge, and get it done soon"

"Not part of our jobs" is like cutting the arrow.

Someone else is like the surgeon.

Or when I say to someone who wants my help, "I totally agree with it, but I have to talk to someone else to make sure".

"Totally agree" is like cutting the arrow.

"Someone else" is the surgeon again.

There are still a lot of examples you need to taste by yourself.

Pan Fixing Way
The cooking pan is broken. You had a pan fixer to fix it.

While the pan fixer is scratching the black dirt off the bottom of the pan, he says to you, "Please make some fire for me."

When you turn your back to him, he hit the pan a few times, then the crack on the pan gets bigger.

Then he tells you, "Look, the crack on this pan is so long.

You couldn't see it if I didn't scratch the dirt off.

Now I have to put more nails in it."

Then you look and say, "Great! I'm so happy I found you, or the pan wouldn't work without you!"

After it's done the pan fixer and the pan owner are all happy in the end.

There are so many affairs in history that went like this.

Some say, "Many of the Chinese revolutions – they cut the good part and cured it."

This is the "pan fixing way".

In the Qing dynasty, people mostly used arrow cutting way.

After that, people used both arrow cutting and pan fixing way.

The 2 ways above are examples of doing things, no matter when and where.

It will be successful if you use it right, and it will fail if you don't use it.

Guangzhong was a great politician in Chinese history. He made things in these 2 ways.

Diren crusaded against the Qei. Qi (empire) waited.

After Diren beat down Wei, Qi came out and said "Have to keep it even if we lose everything".

This is pan fixing way. In the war of Zhaolin, he didn't blame Chu emperor about usurping him, but blames that he didn't pay the tribute he had to.

This is the arrow cutting way.

At that time, the Chu empire was so much stronger than Qi.

Guangzhong asked QI Huangong to crusade against the Chu.

You can say he broke the pan to fix it.

And when the Chu tried to fight, he cut the arrow right away.

The war of Zhaolin started with pan fixing, and ended with arrow cutting.

He could fix the broken pan – that's why he was called "The great genius".

Wang Dao was the prime minister in Jin Dynasty.

There was a traitor at that time. Wang Dao didn't go catch him.

Tao Kan blamed him, and he answered, "I'm just waiting for the good time to attack."

Kan laughed and said, "He was just waiting for the traitor to become stronger."

Wang Dao's "Good time waiting" is like keeping the top of the arrow, and waiting for the surgeon.

Many big men were crying in Xinting. Wang Dao changed colors and said, "We should get together and revive our empire.

Why are we crying here as the prisoners of Chu?"

He acted like he was doing it for justice, picked up the hammer and tried to fix the pan, but he just didn't mean to do anything.

The two emperors, Huai and Min were left North, and could never come back again.

The arrow was never taken out.
Wang Dao's action is kind of like Guan Zhong.

That's why he was called the "Guan Zhong on the other side of the river (Jiang Zuo Yiwu)".

If you followed what I said, you should have been a great politician.

Conclusion

I have said so much until now, at this moment we are waiting for the big melon we grew.

I have to tell the readers that:

While using Thick Black Theory we have to put some moral cover over it.

We cannot show it directly.

The reason why Wang Mang failed was because people knew he was black and thick too much.

If he didn't show so much, I'm afraid he would still be eating cold pork in Confucius's temple.

Hanfe Zi said, "Tell people that you dislike it, but use it behind their back."

This is a necessary way too.

Like the book you are reading now, you should hide it under your pillow. Not on the table.

And if somebody asks if you know Li Zongwu, you should say seriously, "That guy was the most terrible person! He was talking about Thick and Black. I shouldn't have known him."

But you should treat Li Zongwu as a master who "enlightens your way to success".

I believe you will have a wonderful career in front of you, and you will be eating cold pork in Confucius's temple.

And every time when I hear somebody criticizing me, I will be glad and say, "My idea is on the road."

What I said about Thick Black Theory is that: "We should put some moral cover over Thick Black Theory".

I mean to the moral people.

If you met somebody who studies sex, I guess it's not interesting for him to talk about morality.

And now, you should put the "love is holy" cover on it.

If you met a friend of Marx, you should put the cover of "the people are everything".

He would probably call you "comrade".

Anyway, we need to put on some kind of cover, which is also something we need to learn.

Anytime, anywhere, every way to success is around

Thick Black Theory.

You should think about it more if you really want to learn.

Appendix 1

The Thirty Six Thick Black Strategies

I. 勝 戰 計 Stratagems when in a superior position

Fool the Emperor to Cross the Sea
This Ji has often been mis-translated as fool the sky, or fool heaven to cross the sea.

However, the literal meaning is to fool the Emperor.

In ancient China, the emperor was regarded as the "Son of Heaven".

Fooling the emperor to cross the sea simple means to hide your true intentions.

Don't hide your activity, because then you will be suspect.

Instead, hide your true activities behind a feint.

Besiege Wei to Rescue Zhao
If your opponent is to strong to attack directly, attack him at a weak point.

Those weak points could be things, people or places which they care about.

It's important to keep in mind that every human, no matter how invincible they may seem has points of vulnerability.

Kill with a Borrowed Sword
If you can't successfully attack an enemy, use someone else to attack him.

For example – Trick one of his allies into attacking him.

Create traitors within his midst, or use his own strength against him.

Await the Exhausted Enemy at Your Ease
Don't allow your opponent to choose the time or the place for a confrontation.

You should choose both the space and time for engaging your opponent.

Force him to use his energy on wasted efforts while conserving your own energy.

When he's exhausted and confused attack with power and purpose.

Loot a Burning House
When your opponent is dealing with internal conflict, attack.

Clamor in the East, Attack in the West
Attack where your opponent least expects it.

Create false expectations in your opponents mind by using feints.

II. 敵 戰 計 Stratagems for confrontation

Create Something From Nothing
In fighting, use the same feint twice.

Your opponent will be afraid to react to the third similar feint.

However, the third feint is the actual attack.

Openly Repair The Walkway, Secretly March to Chencang
Attack your opponent with two converging forces.

The first attack should be direct and obvious.

The second attack is sneaky and unexpected, causing him to divide his forces at the last minute.

Observe the Fire on the Opposite Shore
Avoid going into battle until all the players are exhausted from fighting each other.

Go in with full strength and pick up the pieces.

Hide Your Dagger Behind a Smile
Gain your enemies trust while secretly moving against him.

Sacrifice the Plum Tree In Place of the Peach

Sacrifice short term objectives in the interest of obtaining long term goals.

Beat The Grass To Startle The Snake
If you can't see your enemies plan run a short, direct attack.

His reaction will show his strategy.

III. 攻戰計 Stratagems for attack

Borrow a Corpse to Raise the Spirit
Revive something from the past and give it a new purpose or new meaning.

These could include:
- old institutions
- old technology
- old methods

Lure the Tiger Down the Mountain
Don't attack a well entrenched opponent.

Lure him from his stronghold and separate him from the source of his strength.

To Catch Something, First Let It Go
A cornered opponent will always fight more desperately.

Make him believe he still has a chance for freedom and in the end when his morale is low he will surrender more easily.

Toss Out A Brick To Attract Jade
Create an illusion of opportunity.

To Catch the Bandits First Capture Their Leader

In order to capture, weaken or destroy an opponents forces, focus on attacking their leader.

Steal The Firewood From Under the Pot
Undermine your opponents foundation. Attack the source of his power.

IV. 混 戰 計 Stratagems for confused situations

Trouble The Water To Catch The Fish
Create confusion to weaken your opponents perception and judgment.

Do something unusual, strange or unexpected. A distracted enemy is more vulnerable.

Shed Your Skin Like the Golden Cicada
If you are in danger of defeat, create an illusion.

Move your forces away behind the facade.

Shut the Door to Catch the Thief
Capture your enemy quickly if possible. If they flee, don't pursue.

Befriend a Distant Enemy to Attack One Nearby
Bordering nations often become enemies while distant nations make for good allies.

Borrow the Road to Conquer Guo
Borrow the resources of an ally to defeat an opponent.

Once your opponent is defeated, turn the resources back against the ally.

Replace The Beams With Rotten Timbers

Force your opponent to react differently than he was trained to.

V. 併戰計 Stratagems for gaining ground

Point At The Mulberry But Curse The Locust Tree

Discipline, control or warn people who you can't directly confront using allegory and innuendo.

If you don't name names they can't respond without revealing themselves publicly.

Feign Madness But Keep Your Balance

Create confusion about your intentions and motivations.

Make your opponent underestimate your ability.

When he drops his guard, attack.

Lure Your Enemy Onto the Roof, Then Take Away the Ladder

Use bait and tricks to lure your enemy onto dangerous ground.

Cut off his lines of communications and means of escape.
Your opponent must fight both you and the dangerous ground.

Tie Silk Blossoms to the Dead Tree

Make something of no value seem valuable.

Make something of no threat seem dangerous.

Make something of no use seem useful.

Exchange the Role of Guest for that of Host
Infiltrate your opponent's camp using cooperation, surrender and peace treaties.

Discover his weakness and attack the source of his strength.

The Strategy of Beautiful Women
Send beautiful women to your opponent to weaken his will and create discord and jealousy in his camp.

VI. 敗 戰 計 Stratagems for desperate situations

The Strategy of Open City Gates
If you know you are going to lose stop preparing to fight and act casually in the hopes that you can trick your enemy into believing you have more power or are more prepared than you actually are.

The Strategy of Sowing Discord
Destroy your opponents ability to fight by creating discord with his allies, advisers, family, commanders, soldiers, and people.

While he's repairing these relationships attack.

The Strategy of Injuring Yourself
Pretend to be injured to make your opponent drop his guard.

Pretend a mutual enemy injured you to get close to him.

The Tactic of Combining Tactics
Combine tactics as necessary.

If All Else Fails Retreat

Did you enjoy this book? Want more...?

Master Your Life At Every Level – RIGHT NOW!

I'm always interested in helping people with transforming and improving their lives and would love to stay in touch and keep you up to date with the latest news! Check out my other books and material and follow me for additional support and training!

- **Website:** http://www.earthwaterfireair.com

- **Facebook:** http://www.facebook.com/thefourelementssystem

- **Twitter:** http://www.twitter.com/thickblack

The Way Of Strategy

The advanced manual on The Art Of Strategic Thinking, by Jon Anxin which helps you win every time - without fear or guilt!

In The Way Of Strategy you'll learn to master The Art Of Strategic Thinking

And Mental Warfare in an easy, step by step way that you can begin applying right now to every area of your life.

You're about to uncover the simple strategic framework that has proven itself to be effective, time and time again – for over 3,000 years...

Whether you need to gain more influence in your personal or business life, begin or complete an important project or even if you may someday need to fight in a real life violent struggle – you'll find these simple and easy to use principles to not only be a lifesaver, but – they may LITERALLY save your life!

[CLICK HERE TO DOWNLOAD THE WAY OF STRATEGY NOW](#)

The Way Of The Sage

In this no-holds-barred training manual, Jonathan Anxin provides a complete overview of his own self-awakening, as well as a step by step process which has worked for other awakeners for thousands of years.

Don't be fooled by Wu-peddlers who want to sell you a false view of enlightenment or so-called spirituality...

Most of the so-called "spiritual" community has it completely wrong, because there are no butterfly experts in the caterpillar world.

If you're ready to achieve true liberation, enlightenment and awakening, there is only one framework by which to do that.

In The Way Of The Sage you'll discover exactly what the framework is, and uncover a simple, step by step process, that — if followed will result in your own permanent awakening.

[Click Here To Download The Way Of The Sage](#)

Thick Black Theory

"Thick Black Theory Will Show You How To WIN EVERY TIME Without Fear, Anger Or Guilt."

Don't settle for second-class knock off copies, the original Thick Black Theory contains the secrets that you can best use to Gain Massive Power, Fast!

What Is Thick Black Theory?

"Li Zongwu, a disgruntled politician published it in 1911, a year of chaos in China when Sun Yat Sen overthrew the Ching Dynasty and set up the Chinese Republic.

Li was a scientist of political intrigue.

He writes: 'When you conceal your will from others, that is Thick. When you impose your will on others, that is Black.' Thick Black Theory describes the ruthless, hypocritical means men use to obtain and hold power. It went through several printings before being banned as subversive." –SUCCESS MAGAZINE

This is the first and only translation of Li Zongwu's seminal work on "black" strategy.

Thick Black Theory is a classic treatise on strategy, similar to Sun Tzu's The Art Of War.

Anyone Who loves The Art Of War, Machiavelli, The 48 Laws Of Power, Etc. Will Also Love Thick Black Theory.

CLICK HERE TO DOWNLOAD THICK BLACK THEORY NOW

White Lotus Revolution

Banned For Hundreds Of Years, The Original Teachings Of The White Lotus Society from China, or the "Bailian Jings..."

This material brings to light the banned teachings of the White Lotus society which explain:

- The Ultimate Nature Of Reality
- The Hidden History Of Religions
- The Great Conspiracy Of History

Jonathan Anxin also provides full instructions for the practice of White Lotus, including the Dragon Flower Meeting. This material has been banned in China, and much of it has been banned for the past 800 years.

This work has not been translated into English or outside of the Chinese language previously, and is the only source to get a high level understanding of not only White Lotus Society, but also Taoism, Buddhism, Christianity, Confucianism and Islam.

CLICK HERE TO DOWNLOAD WHITE LOTUS REVOLUTION NOW

Printed in Great Britain
by Amazon